FAIL-SAFE LEADERSHIP

STRAIGHT TALK ABOUT CORRECTING THE LEADERSHIP CHALLENGES IN YOUR ORGANIZATION

BY
Linda L. Martin
&
Dr. David G. Mutchler

FAIL-SAFE
LEADERSHIP

STRAIGHT TALK ABOUT
CORRECTING THE LEADERSHIP
CHALLENGES IN YOUR ORGANIZATION

DELTA BOOKS
ORLANDO, FLORIDA 32862

FAIL-SAFE LEADERSHIP

All rights reserved. Published by Delta Books, P.O. Box 621111,
Orlando, Florida 32862.

Printed in the United States of America
3 4 5 6 7 8 9 0

Library of Congress Control Number: 2001097771

Mutchler, David G.
    Fail-Safe Leadership: straight talk about correcting
    the leadership challenges in your organization
    /David G. Mutchler, Linda L. Martin.
    ISBN 0-9715732-1-2
    1. Leadership. 2. Results. 3. Organizational Change.
    I. Martin, Linda L.   II. Title.

2001 . . . . 1st Printing
2002 . . . . 2nd Printing
2003 . . . . 3rd Printing

Acknowledgments

It would be difficult to thank everyone individually who contributed to this work, as the list would be long. Certainly to be singled out are Cindy Shaw and Gary Bohanick of Resource Associates Corporation for their superb work in graphic design, layout, and production. A special thanks goes to Paul R. Kehoe of Leadership Development Systems, LLC for serving in the role of project manager for the book. It was his ability to oversee and coordinate the many facets of moving a book from start to finish that helped ensure its timely delivery and ultimate quality.

DEDICATION

To the many talented
executives and managers
for whom we've worked over the
years, and from whom we've
learned the various parts that
make up the whole.

CONTENTS

Note
To avoid using the masculine gender exclusively
where referring to both males and females in the
workplace, we have randomly used masculine and
feminine pronouns throughout the book.

FOREWORD

In my thirty-some years of experience in management and consulting with both large and small corporations of every conceivable ilk, I have observed a growing trend that there is an overabundance of managers and a huge lack of leaders. This situation clearly has a negative impact on an organization's ability to grow and to compete. It seems to beg a crucial question: If leadership is so critical to an organization's success, why, then, isn't there more of it? In exploring this question I have made several general observations concerning leadership; and to my delight, I was pleased to see that most of them have been succinctly addressed in this book.

The first of those observations is that leaders come in different ages, genders, roles, profiles, nationalities, behavioral styles, etc. There really is no "one size fits all" prototype for a leader, which explains why so many attempts at leadership training continue to fail.

Second, there are some practices and processes which successful leaders understand and implement. One of these is their ability to comprehend the big picture and translate that understanding into specific, measurable goals that are cascaded down throughout the organization. Such a "goal alignment process" serves two important functions, namely: (a) it has the impact of inspiring and energizing the entire organization by focusing everyone on the steps needed to achieve results; and (b) it serves as a process to deal with the inevitability of near-term change required to produce long-term results.

Congruent with this, the authors have spelled out an extremely effective alignment process in this timely book. I have found that whenever this particular organizational alignment process is put into effect, it not only provides valuable direction to a company, it also creates an environment where leaders seem to blossom from within and throughout the organization. The beauty of it is that when leaders focus on process, they become keenly aware that it is the people and the alignment of their activities, behaviors, and attitudes that make the overall plan happen.

In this well-written, quick-read book, you will gain valuable understanding of these key issues, along with many other important insights. It is clear that the authors did not intend to present a step-by-step guide that would become the end-all on how to become a successful leader. It is, rather, a refreshingly new and dynamic perspective on the whole subject of leadership that will open some helpful doors for you to get started on the right path to solving your leadership problems.

Those who decide to take the challenge will find considerable benefit both personally and professionally from doing so. In my experience, the principles that the authors have laid out are universal. They work in government, sole proprietorships, family owned companies, large corporations, departments within organizations, not-for-profits, volunteer organizations, and even in one's personal life. Their approach is logical and well tested. In a word, it "works." Anyone who takes their message seriously will find themselves indebted to the authors, as have I, for having shared their insights on such a vital subject.

JAMES B. GODSHALL,
President, Total Quality Institute

(Mr. Godshall is an internationally recognized business leader and author of continuous quality improvement materials that are used throughout the world.)

CHAPTER 1

INTRODUCTION

Few subjects receive more attention in business today than that of leadership. The reason is that leadership is the critical linchpin that holds today's organization together while preparing it for the change and evolution necessary to succeed in these turbulent and challenging times.

Turbulent times, indeed! Technological advancements have accelerated the rate of change to near warp speed. With that speed of change we are seeing unprecedented challenges: commoditization of the market, unbelievably fierce competition, and for many companies, rapidly diminishing profits. Wall Street, for example, continues to report earnings for many companies that are less than expected. Well-established companies continue to lose market share, and huge multi-nationals are being surpassed by young startup organizations that are more responsive, customer-focused, and flexible.

As a result, leadership is now challenged on a regular basis with layoffs, flattening organizational structures, expanding skill requirements, new channels of doing business, the challenge of retaining the best people, more work falling on the shoulders of fewer and fewer people, and the list goes on. And of course, it all has to be done faster than ever before.

While there is no magical answer to any of these issues, much less all of them, certain themes nevertheless emerge in this business environment that become absolutely necessary for survival. Among them are leadership, teamwork, alignment, empowerment, accountability, speed to market, and quality. At the top of the list—uncontested—is *leadership*. One need not look far for experts who say as much.

- Warren Bennis in *Managing People Is Like Herding Cats* says that, "Around the globe, **we currently face... a deepening leadership crisis in organizations.** Unlike the possibility of plague or nuclear holocaust, the leadership crisis will probably not become the basis for a best-seller or a blockbuster movie, but in many ways it is the **most urgent and dangerous** of the threats we face today, if only because it is insufficiently recognized and little understood."

- Fred Fiedler and Martin Chemers in *Improving Leadership Effectiveness* state, "The quality of leadership, **more than any other single factor,** determines the success or failure of an organization."

- Brian Tracy in *The 100 Absolutely Unbreakable Laws of Business Success* points out that "Leadership is **the most important single factor** in determining business success or failure in our competitive, turbulent, fast-moving economy." He goes on to say there has never been a greater need for leaders at all levels than there is today.

~

Most top executives are aware that such claims about leadership as put forth by these and other experts ring true in their respective organizations every day. They tell us this all the time. "There's a dearth of leadership in our company." "I pay good money to hire top leaders—why can't they lead?" "I have to admit that we have a real shortage of leadership in our company today."

That having been said, there is another harsh reality that must be faced, as well. *Regardless of where you are as an executive and regardless of your organization's position in the marketplace, nothing you have done thus far ensures your success in the future.* Only one thing will, and that one thing is the very challenge facing you today: *You must find a way to develop a fail-safe system of leadership in your company that helps you lead your organization to unprecedented levels of success and achievement.*

"How is this done?" becomes the obvious question of the day. Proposed solutions are diverse, and often complicated. Most of the executives we've worked with have told us at the outset that efforts to correct their leadership challenges have been random and piecemeal. One initiative barely gets rolling when the next leadership "flavor of the year" takes its place. These and similar confessions are living testaments to the difficulty of finding and utilizing a comprehensive and effective approach to fixing the crux of our corporate leadership problems.

People are not to be faulted for this, mind you, since viable solutions are difficult to find. But they do exist, and **that's exactly what this book is about.** It is, in short, straight talk devoid of theoretical fluff for those who are tired of poring through book after book, or attending seminar after seminar, in search of what to DO to fix their leadership problems, only to find yet one more theory on what the nature of the problem is.

~

There are three points to note before reading on. First, the book is obviously brief, which is intentional. We find that most people don't have time to read business books like they once did, as other demands on their time have become too great. Out of respect for the reader, we've followed the principle of parsimony by applying Ockham's Razor to keep things as absolutely simple and brief as possible without diluting the power of the message. It is a quick read with a powerful punch, a punch that could well make a real difference for you both in your career and in your organization.

Second, the message presented here does not provide you with instant or easy answers. Let's face it, there *are* no easy answers when it comes to leadership-related issues. But the fact that there are not instant or easy answers does not mean that there are not *effective* answers. And that is what this book does. It provides you with effective answers that will enhance your leadership knowledge and awareness, and as a result, help you create an action plan that will ensure continued success.

Third, make no mistake about it, this is not your typical book about leadership. If the world of leadership is going West today, this book heads due East. It is a 180 degree turn regarding most of the assumptions that currently exist about leadership. Retired Army Colonel Dandridge M. Malone once said, "The very essence of leadership is its purpose. And the purpose of leadership is to accomplish a task. That is what leadership *does*—and what it *does* is more important than what it is and how it works."

We say, EXACTLY! That's why this book is not so much about what leadership is, or about how it works. It is about what leadership DOES! Period. End of sentence. In the words of Peter Drucker, *"Leadership is all about results."* So is this book. We are excited about what this can mean to the success of your organization!

— QUESTIONS TO ASK YOURSELF —

1. In your opinion, what role does leadership play in the success of your organization?

2. On a scale of 1 to 10 (10 being highest), how would you rate the overall effectiveness of leadership in your company today?

3. What would it mean to your organization if your rating were to rise 1 point? 2 points?

4. What is the risk if you answered anything lower than 10?

CHAPTER 2

A QUICK TEMPERATURE CHECK

Business today has taken on many new dimensions. Our leaders are faced with more challenges, more choices, and more opportunities than ever before. Profit margins are shrinking, new markets are emerging, the workplace is changing, and competition is threatening even the largest corporations.

In the face of these many changes, the ability to develop fail-safe leadership throughout your organization is far and away your most competitive advantage. As the most important single factor in determining success or failure in your organization, leadership is the foundation upon which you are able to create sustained success. As you may appreciate, it is one of the top issues that more and more organizations are evaluating.

Regardless of the current state of your business, then, it is imperative that you ask yourself the question, "Might the leadership in **my** company be failing?" A valuable tool to help you determine the answer to this question is the following checklist. The answer may be "yes" if one or more of these conditions are present in your organization:

- ❏ Excessive meetings
- ❏ Preponderance of consensus-driven decision making
  (i.e. a cover-your-behind mentality)
- ❏ Lack of personal accountability
- ❏ Time consuming and/or meaningless performance evaluations
- ❏ Communication problems

- ❑ Difficulty terminating poor performers
- ❑ Misalignment/lack of coordinated effort
- ❑ Personality conflicts and/or power struggles
- ❑ Difficulty keeping employees motivated
- ❑ Unacceptable results
- ❑ Time management problems
- ❑ Reactive rather than proactive thinking
- ❑ Micro-management
- ❑ Can't-do attitudes
- ❑ Chronically sagging sales
- ❑ Unproductive teams and/or ineffective teamwork
- ❑ Duplication of effort
- ❑ High staff turnover
- ❑ Failure to achieve quality standards
- ❑ Fear of making decisions

PLEASE NOTE

If any of these conditions exist in your company, this does **not** mean that you, the reader, are an ineffective leader. It simply means that your company has leadership problems.

~

You may find yourself wondering as many people do what this checklist has to do with leadership, per se. Here's the connection. Organizations are complex and dynamic entities. The larger the organization, the more this is true. Because it is difficult to comprehend the corporate entity in its totality, there is a strong tendency, both from inside and from outside the organization, to assess corporate problems based on what they *appear* to be rather than on their deeper causations.

When leadership in a company falls short, that shortfall reflects itself in any one or more of a whole complex of problems—the very same problems, in fact, which you see in the checklist. The presence of any one of these is cause for concern because, like rodents, one does not likely exist by itself in isolation. Where there is one, there are usually many.

Obviously, the more of these problems that are present in your company, the greater the chance that leadership challenges exist, and therefore the greater the need to remedy the situation in order to ensure continued success.

∿

Another way to look at this is to liken leadership deficiencies to a disease or illness. Most diseases or illnesses rarely reveal themselves as such. Instead, they disguise their true nature by wearing various masks, called "symptoms." The checklist represents the more common symptoms of deficient leadership in organizations.

The secret to optimal health is to treat the core problem rather than focus on isolated symptoms. This same principle is true with leadership challenges. For too long we have tried to solve our leadership problems by applying a bandage when major surgery was needed in order to exact a cure. Such a paradigm shift—from "bandage" to "surgery" mentality—will require that we begin thinking in terms, again, of "causes" rather than isolated issues or situations.

Doing so for many people is a new perspective. Traditionally, for example, few people would associate many of the items on the checklist—e.g. excessive meetings, outdated performance evaluations, or poor time management—with having a leadership problem. But you will learn that every symptom on the checklist, without exception, is a direct outgrowth of a deficiency in leadership.

Once you understand that one or more of these various symptoms indicate deeper leadership problems, you can begin to implement the real solution. You will see that leadership is about the processes that do or do not exist in your organization, processes which ensure that leadership accomplishes what it is supposed to accomplish.

Think of leadership as a bicycle wheel. The outer rim represents desired results. The center of the wheel, or hub, represents leadership. The spokes connecting the hub to the outer rim represent the leadership processes necessary to achieve the desired results. Missing, broken, and bent spokes all stand for leadership problems—roadblocks, bottlenecks, and obstacles to achieving desired outcomes.

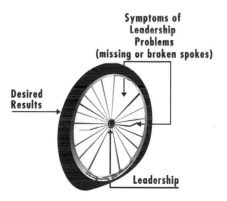

Symptoms of Leadership Problems (missing or broken spokes)

Desired Results →

Leadership

How many spokes can be missing or damaged (that is, how many symptoms must exist) before results are compromised? One? Two? Five?

Clearly, a fully functioning bicycle wheel requires that ALL of its parts function at full capacity. Just one spoke missing begins to reduce the overall effectiveness of the unit.

So it is with companies. The presence of merely one of the aforementioned symptoms gives warning that your company may have leadership challenges. An accumulation of them—over time and uncorrected—could result in achieving far less than the outcomes you desire.

— QUESTIONS TO ASK YOURSELF —

1. Have you ever had the thought: "I know just what I need my people to do, but they can't seem to get it done"?

2. If yes, why do you think this is the case?

3. What would the benefit be to your company if this situation could be remedied?

CHAPTER 3

THE OLD GRAY MARE, SHE AIN'T WHAT SHE USED TO BE

Leadership "ain't what it used to be," either, although by and large most companies continue to act every day as if it were. Sadly, many organizations are operating with an eighteenth or nineteenth century mind-set about leadership, yet expecting twenty-first century results.

In truth, the quality of the leadership within your company is the only sustaining competitive advantage you have in today's global arena. And the reality is that no business can survive and succeed unless their leadership is current with the times. This means that it must be prepared to shoulder the unprecedented challenges faced by virtually every organization today.

The first critical step toward fixing the leadership challenges in your company, then, is to gain a full understanding of how our entire notion of leadership must change for it to become fail-safe. Join us as we facilitate a seminar on Leadership Development to see better what we mean.

∼

It is day one in the opening minutes of a meeting with ten Vice Presidents in the room, each of whom represent a different company. They are about to participate in an exercise that is designed to create an enhanced understanding of what it takes to be a leader today.

It goes like this. First we ask them to think of someone, separately, whom they consider to be an effective leader. Once they've written down the name of the individual they've selected, we then ask them to think of three qualities about that person which caused him or her to be selected as a strong leader.

> NOTE: Before you continue reading, you might want to take a minute and do this same exercise yourself. Think of someone you consider to be an ideal leader. What are the top three attributes that they exhibit as a leader?

Once everyone has listed the top three characteristics of the leader of their choice, we then compare their lists. Imagine that you were participating in the meeting. Would you guess that their lists closely resemble each other or that they're markedly different? Here are their actual answers:

◆

patient
unemotional
detached and able to see the big picture

◆

ability to stand tough
communicative
ability to relate to diverse situations

◆

decisive
visionary
good teacher

◆

influential
decisive
good listener

◆

inspiring
good negotiator
good delegator

◆

understanding
knowledgeable
humanitarian

◆

decisive
encourages working together
intelligent

◆

driven
demanding
passionate about his beliefs

◆

energetic
caring
not easily persuaded by others

◆

involved
willing to do what she asks of others
listens to other's ideas

This list is typical of the many we've helped facilitate. Not all lists contain the exact same attributes, of course. And there is usually some small degree of overlap; "decisive" appears three times, for example. But what is far more important to notice is that the list in total names a *wide* range of leadership characteristics, many of which are significantly different from the others.

We ask the group, "What does it mean that there are so many differences?" "Which characteristics are the 'true' leadership qualities?" "Will the real leader please stand up?"

"All of them are true," someone says. "But how can that be," we ask, "when some of the qualities are practically opposites of others—*passionate* versus *unemotional,* for example, or *demanding* versus *understanding*? Or what about *involved* versus *detached and able to see the big picture?*"

"Hmmmm," someone says, as if voicing the temporary confusion of the group.

Then momentary silence, pause for reflection. So we ask, "Is there any one thing about each of these individuals that they all have in common which may not have yet been listed?" Then after a few moments someone says it. "Each of them is (or was) successful in his or her own right." We ask what this means. "Each of them is (or was) able to set goals and reach the results they wanted to achieve." They all agree.

So we ask that they please explain their comments further.

- A former high school basketball coach led his teams to many championships.

- A current CEO drives corporate profits beyond expectations year after year.

- By encouraging her students to a higher education, a former teacher impacted the lives of many students who would otherwise not have gone to college.

- A general led his troops to victory against unbelievable odds.

- A manager is able to keep her staff continuously motivated to perform beyond expectations.

What is particularly interesting about this exercise is that no one, whether in this group or any other, ever picks a "loser," which is to say someone who didn't or doesn't GET RESULTS. For example, no one ever picks the general who lost the war, the ex-coach who rarely won any games, or the CEO whose company loses profits year after year. Regardless of the role, title, or occupation,

> **What makes any person a leader is his or her ability to set goals and ACHIEVE DESIRED RESULTS— nothing more, nothing less.**

The behavioral characteristics that we typically associate with "leadership," such as good delegator, visionary, etc., are of secondary importance. In fact, they are of *little* significance except to the extent that they contribute to getting desired outcomes.

~

This, then, is the first principle you must embrace in order to shore up the leadership difficulties in your company: *your definition of leadership must change if you plan to keep pace with the times.* Short of doing so, your leadership may be hopelessly destined to fail because, like the proverbial house built on sand, its very definition is built on a weak foundation.

Leadership is no longer about possessing certain personal characteristics, but rather about the ability to set goals and achieve desired results. More specifically, *leadership* is about doing those things that *lead* to getting results.

Making this shift in thinking is the cornerstone upon which you will be able to ensure that the leadership in your organization will be safe from failing in the future. It is the very same cornerstone upon which the remainder of this book is built.

— QUESTIONS TO ASK YOURSELF —

1. Have you generally thought about leadership in terms of the attributes an individual has?

2. Can you relate to Peter Drucker's statement that "Leadership is all about results"?

3. Are you ready to embrace a results-based model of leadership that gets your company efficiently and effectively to where you want it to be?

CHAPTER 4

A ROUND WORLD MAKES FOR BETTER SAILING

As most school-aged children can tell us, the pervasive belief about the earth before 1492 was that it was flat. Sailors dared not venture out of sight from land for fear of falling off the edge into nothingness. All of navigation was defined by, and limited to, the parameters of that belief. As a result, oceans were not explored, and new lands remained undiscovered.

Then one day Columbus challenged the conventional wisdom by suggesting from his evidence that the world was really round. Based on his new definition, he courageously set sail, and as a result discovered America. In doing so, he revolutionized the world by creating new opportunities to explore horizons as yet unknown.

~

For many years sports experts felt that no one would ever break the four-minute mile. Even physiologists thought that the mind and the body had reached their limits. Roger Bannister, however, challenged that definition and as a result, realized his dream of running the mile in less than four minutes. In doing so, he opened the doors for athletes in every field to reach records that had been previously thought impossible to achieve.

~

Such is the nature, and *power,* of all definitions. They shape our logic by imposing limits that must conform to the boundaries of the definition itself.

This same principle, that *definitions shape and limit our reality,* applies equally to the concept of "leadership development." Define a leader as we have become accustomed to—someone who possesses a certain set of personal attributes—and developing leaders will subsequently mean little else than attempting to develop these personal leadership characteristics in individuals. Challenge that definition of leadership to mean "the ability to get results," however, and a whole new world of possibilities for **developing** leaders in our organizations opens wide.

~

Before we discuss the popular current paradigm about leadership development in any detail, it is important to acknowledge that for ages it was assumed that leaders are best developed by "promoting from within." The practice was, and for many companies still is, to select people and promote them into leadership assignments based on their performance in a previous position. The unstated rule was, promote our "super" workers to supervisors and then sit back and wait for them to "lead."

It is not surprising, of course, that often they didn't, and don't, lead! Their competence in a "worker" role in no way ensures that they will be successful in a "leadership" role. In fact, an unusually high competence as a worker can actually contribute to one's *difficulty* in becoming a successful leader. The reason is that it is much easier and quicker to continue to "do it yourself" rather than train and lead others to perform to the same level of competence.

Said differently, trying to develop leaders by simply promoting from within is too often proof positive of the truth of the

Peter Principle, which purports that in a hierarchy individuals tend to rise to their level of incompetence. The effects from this practice are negative for the individual, the people with whom he or she works, and for the organization. Little wonder that such "leaders" so often fail to lead. And what's worse, a common practice is to continue to promote these people up the corporate ladder! The point is that attempting to develop leaders solely through promotion means there is no guarantee that any real "leading" will happen at all.

~

Over the years, most organizations have come to recognize the weakness inherent in the "promotion" model for developing their leaders. They now understand that while certain individuals may have the potential to excel in a leadership role, they first need to gain certain skills. This is why many organizations usually make a concerted effort to "develop" their leaders beyond simply promoting them. They do this by using what has become in recent years the popular definition of leadership development, namely, *developing individual characteristics in persons who are assigned leadership responsibilities.*

This commonly used definition of leadership development has its roots in what is known as a "competency-based" model. The assumption is that there are certain essential competencies—in this case, designated leadership qualities, such as decisive, inspiring, energetic, and so on—required in all people considered to be effective leaders.

Historically, and mostly still today, a leader is thought of as a person who exhibits these key leadership characteristics. We saw how this assumption was made in the exercise with the ten Vice Presidents in the last chapter. Larger companies often designate a certain number of such qualities to a list that becomes, in effect, their corporate definition of leadership. Some have 22 such characteristics, others 31, others 10 or maybe 40. The exact number is arbitrary depending on what leadership book someone might have read, or what consultant may have given advice on the matter. Or, perhaps it's the work of a task force within the company assigned to research the subject and compile such a list.

Smaller companies more likely send their leaders off to a workshop or seminar on leadership. Here the facilitator in charge presents his list of leadership attributes intended to become the standard toward which those in attendance are expected to measure and develop themselves.

Whether the organization is large or small, whether the definition of leadership was developed in-house or out, the objective is always the same: *use the designated leadership characteristics as a yardstick against which to train and develop all individuals in the company who are in positions of "leadership."* The assumption is, if you grow leadership qualities in people, then somehow this will positively impact corporate results.

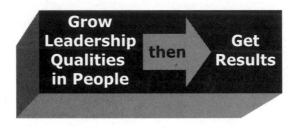

The plain truth is that today's conventional wisdom about leadership development—*that attempting to grow certain characteristics in people which other effective leaders have modeled will somehow lead to results*—is itself now old and suspect. There are two reasons why. First, the impact of such changes on company results is difficult, if not impossible, to measure or track. Second, attempting to change personal leadership attributes in people takes considerable time, which is a luxury we no longer have. Consequently, the "grow leadership qualities in people, then get results" model is fast earning a place alongside the "promotion" model as being out-dated and ineffective.

Times have changed. Business has changed. Competition is brutal and today's margins are slimmer. We are moving at lightning-like speed and all indications are that it will get even tougher and it will happen even faster. A CEO recently shared a comment over lunch that makes this point abundantly clear. He lifted his spoon in front of his face as if to mimic a rear-view mirror, and then said with a choked voice, "One year ago I couldn't even see the competition coming. Today I'm eating their dust!"

The point is that to continue to follow a competency-based model of leadership development in these changed, and changing, times is really to,

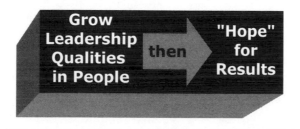

Most people will agree that "hoping" for results in today's tough business environment is simply unacceptable. If we're going to develop leaders sufficient to win in the face of growing business demands, we must let the old definition of leadership development go. Like the promotion model, it, too, is a belief that has simply outlived its logic. What we need is a new and dynamic perspective that is focused on ensuring successful outcomes. What we need in place of a competency-based model for developing leaders, in other words, is a **"results-based"** model.

∿

In a results-based model of leadership development, every attempt to develop people is both defined and justified by the outcome it is intended to achieve. The focus is on results rather than on individual leadership attributes. Defining leadership in this way gives birth to a new and dynamic perspective for how to go about leadership development. Rather than "Grow Leadership Qualities In People, Then *Hope* For Results," it is far more effective to focus on the desired outcomes or results and THEN grow and develop the people and processes to ensure the realization of those results.

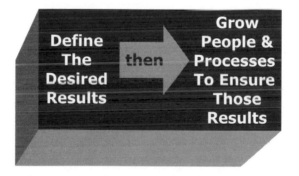

The left side of this equation, **Define The Desired Results,** is not a novel idea. It is, in effect, strategic thinking and business planning, which most companies do periodically in one form or another.

The difficulty is that the strategic business plan is so typically isolated from growing people and processes—the right side of the equation—that rarely do the two ever meet. Consequently, for the vast majority of companies, the business plan— once completed, and often at considerable time and expense—sits on the shelf collecting dust, or is neatly tucked away in a file drawer. It never actually "breathes" and comes to life.

Meanwhile, growing people and developing leaders is addressed as a segregated initiative somewhere else in the organization under the assumption that this will somehow positively impact the strategic plan. Unfortunately, any positive impact that individual leadership development might have on bringing the plan to reality is at best incidental, simply because it is linked neither to the planning process, nor ultimately to the operating model that eventually must bring the plan to completion. All too often, the strategic plan remains a secret, kept from the very people who can ensure its success.

∼

What *is* novel, though, is the right side of the formula—**GROW PEOPLE AND PROCESSES TO ENSURE THE DESIRED RESULTS.** The reason that this model is so powerful is that it links and aligns the vision and strategy with the people and processes that will ensure that the vision is realized.

To better understand this concept, let's reflect for a moment on what it means to "get results" in general. In its most rudimentary form, to get a result is to have a plan or goal, and then to make that goal happen. In the context of organizational success, this means (1) developing a strategic business plan that is focused on the vision of the organization; and (2) aligning the people and processes to ensure its realization. In this way, all operations become linked to the plan such that virtually *everything* that happens in a company works purposefully toward its achievement.

As easy as this is to say, the truth is that the linking of operations to strategy in the vast majority of companies is weak. The reason is that previously the link itself has not been well defined. Now it is. ***Grow People And Processes To Ensure Achieving The Defined Result!***

Doing so is as powerful as it is unique. It is how to make things happen in your organization. It is where the competitive advantage lies today. It is also the very essence of what it means to "develop" your leadership.

~

Once you accept the new definition of leadership as "the ability to get results," *you must next commit to a leadership development process that aggressively grows people and processes to achieve the strategic direction of your company.* By doing so, you effectively convert all efforts to develop your leadership from a competency-based model to a results-based model. This is the only clear, predictable, scientific way to guarantee getting results in today's fast-paced, turbulent economy. Failing to do so is the modern day equivalent of continuing to hold onto the belief that the world is flat, and insisting that our ships stay close to shore.

∿

To better understand the differences between a competency-based model of leadership development and a results-based model, we conclude this chapter with a side-by-side comparison of the two.

Competency-Based Model		Results-Based Model
Traditional Approach	⇨	Leading Edge Approach
Focuses on Personal Characteristics	⇨	Focuses on Results
Training Oriented (Emphasis Is on Imparting New Leadership Skills or Qualities)	⇨	Development Oriented (Optimizes Utilization of Intrinsic and Existing Leadership Characteristics)
Attributes to Be Imparted Are Generalized, Subjective, and Tend to Make Leaders More and More Alike	⇨	Attributes to Be Developed Are Results-Specific, Objective, and Maximize the Qualities Unique to Each Leader
Difficult to Link to Operating Systems	⇨	Links Directly to Operating Systems

Competency-Based Model (continued)		Results-Based Model (continued)
Difficult to Identify Emerging Leaders	⇨	Emerging Leaders Are Easily Identified Based on Ability to Achieve Results
Process of Developing Leaders Is Relatively Slow and Inefficient	⇨	Process of Developing Leaders Is Relatively Fast and Efficient
Assumes Effective Leaders Have Approximately the Same Personal Leadership Characteristics	⇨	Assumes Effective Leaders Vary Considerably With Regard to Personal Leadership Characteristics
No Direct Alignment to Company's Vision and Strategic Plan	⇨	Aligns Directly to Company's Vision and Strategic Plan
Difficult to Measure Against Results	⇨	Easily Measured Against Results

43

Competency-Based Model (continued)		Results-Based Model (continued)
Confusion Deepens Between What Is Expected of Leaders and the Desired Company Results	⇨	Desired Company Results = What Is Expected of Leaders
Link to Company's Bottom Line Is Negligible	⇨	Links Directly to Company's Bottom Line
Difficult to Institutionalize and Deploy Into Various Company Processes	⇨	Institutionalization and Deployment **IS** the Process

— QUESTIONS TO ASK YOURSELF —

1. Developing leadership in a results-based model is quite a different thing than developing leadership in a competency-based model. Can you articulate the differences to yourself?

2. Are you ready to embrace a results-based model of leadership in order to truly get your company to the next level?

CHAPTER 5

TO LEAD OR TO FOLLOW— THAT IS THE QUESTION!

One of the challenges of great leadership is knowing when to lead, when to follow, and when to get out of the way! This may sound like a trite cliché on the surface, but it is absolutely true! One of the revelations of a results-based model of leadership is that, when the focus is on getting results, it becomes apparent that there are times when being a good follower IS being a good leader.

~

Typically when people think of a follower, they think of someone who follows another person, as in the childhood game "follow the leader." But this traditional viewpoint assumes two things: first, that a leader is a person who leads "people"; and second, that followers are "yes-people" who blindly follow along.

By contrast, in our definition of leadership, **a leader is a person who sets goals and achieves results.** She may or may not lead people, and she may or may not follow another person. It all depends on the results she is trying to get. But she always must *follow* effective processes, which is what we mean when we say that,

Every Good Leader Must Be A Good Follower!

NOTE: By "process," we mean in the simplest definition of the term: A way of proceeding with an end in mind; a particular method of doing something, generally involving a certain number of steps or operations that are designed to lead to a particular outcome.

~

Think about it. Accountants follow specific processes to get the results they are employed to get: tax processes, auditing processes, reporting processes, and the like. Winning coaches follow certain processes to build and sustain winning teams: recruiting processes, motivational processes, offensive processes, defensive processes, and so on. Medical professionals follow specific processes to prevent and heal disease: intake processes, physical examination processes, diagnostic processes, surgical processes, and many more. As a general rule of thumb,

> **Successful people are those who are effective at achieving desired outcomes because they follow a predetermined set of processes that *LEAD* to those outcomes.**

This is why successful business leaders spend great quantities of time and money developing their processes for others to follow, *trying* to ensure the realization of their vision: strategic processes, goal-achievement processes, expansion processes, accounting processes, and more.

What we're saying here is that **results-oriented** *leadership development processes* must be added to the list, as well. In fact, given the *supreme* importance of developing your leaders in today's tough business climate, it could well be argued that such processes must be at the *top* of your list of priorities!

~

Some would contend that being good at following a prescribed set of processes that lead to a defined outcome may make a person a good worker, a productive person, a valuable employee, and/or a reliable and successful member of the team. But it does not by itself make one an effective leader.

By the traditional definition of leadership, this argument clearly would be true. That paradigm would suggest there are only select few leaders, and many more— the masses—who follow those few leaders.

It also suggests that the emphasis is on leading people rather than following processes that *lead* to well-defined outcomes. Under this conventional definition, leadership effectiveness is measured against an individual's ability to get others to "follow the leader." The better one is at getting people to follow him, the more effective a leader he is thought to be. And, the better one is at following his or her leader, the more one is perceived as being a good "corporate soldier."

By contrast, a results-based definition of leadership is not about following a person. *It is about following a prescribed set of proven processes that lead to clearly defined results.* In this definition, EVERYONE in your company can be—and ought to be—a leader, because everyone is focused on following the processes that *lead* to the desired outcomes.

It is interesting that in recent years, business executives have been increasingly crying out for how to make everyone in their company a leader, as times like these demand. Yet this would be absolutely impossible to accomplish using the traditional definition of leadership. Who would the leaders lead? The answer for how to do so is implicit in this new definition of leadership, however: *everyone must follow processes that are specifically designed to* **lead** *to prescribed outcomes.* When *everyone* does this, everyone is a leader!

∿

So, is it ever again appropriate to lead people and have followers follow? Of course it is. It all depends on what one is trying to accomplish, what result one is wanting to achieve. If the desired outcome involves influencing people, then one follows the processes that *lead* to influencing people. When it happens that one's personality is conducive to that end, then all the better, but personality is **not** the real point. Behavior that follows key leadership *processes* is the defining issue.

51

Similarly, if the desired result is to accomplish a project, then one follows those processes that *lead* to the successful completion of that project. If one has personal qualities that are helpful toward that end, then again, all the better. But those personal qualities are *always* secondary to what is of paramount importance, namely, the processes which are involved.

Please note that we keep italicizing the word *"lead."* Each instance signals and embodies the spirit of what leadership is all about:

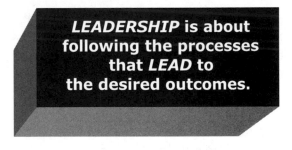

LEADERSHIP is about
following the processes
that **LEAD** to
the desired outcomes.

In other words, the relationship between leadership processes and results is causal: do *this,* and *that* will happen.

∾

The processes required to link a company's operating model with its strategic business plan are ones that we refer to as the **Leadership Development Processes.** They are designed specifically to help you reach the results that you want your company to achieve. They are proven, and they work.

Furthermore, by implementing these processes in your company, you will find that certain individuals will naturally rise to the top to lead your organization forward. In particular, those people who are results oriented will seize the opportunity to embrace and implement these same processes. Such individuals are your true leaders, your leaders of leaders, your people who will achieve the result of helping others get the results you want for your company.

∼

To sum up: If the leadership in your company is failing, your first responsibility, you will recall, is to make the shift in how you define leadership—from personal attributes to the ability to set goals and achieve results. By reconfiguring the definition of leadership in this way, you open exciting new horizons for how to go about **developing** leadership in your company, especially as it relates to linking your vision with operations.

The second step is identifying those processes that will ensure that you take specific action to create results-based leaders within your organization. **One of the single biggest reasons why leaders fail to lead is the absence of effective Leadership Development Processes that ALLOW them to lead.** *All such processes must be carefully and purposely designed, (a) to develop a clear* *strategic direction for your company, and (b) to link your operating systems with that strategic direction in order to ensure achieving the desired results.*

Your third step is to initiate the implementation and institutionalization of these crucial Leadership Development Processes, the two most essential of which are explained in Chapters 6 and 7.

— Questions to Ask Yourself —

1. Do you have Leadership Development Processes in place for your people to follow in order to get the results you desire?

2. List the benefits to your organization if you had such processes working for you.

CHAPTER 6

UNITED
WE STAND,
DIVIDED
WE FALL

The first essential process that needs to be implemented if your company is to become results-based is that of "alignment." Alignment is not a new concept. In fact, it has become somewhat of a buzzword in the corporate world in recent years.

Alignment is a multifaceted concept, and can relate to any number of company functions. It is literally the act of "lining things up." For example, one can align company values, processes to conform to those values, strategies, missions, goals, competencies, training initiatives, and so on. Alignment is important throughout the organization, and all of these applications of the term can certainly add value to a company.

It is not our intention here to restate that which has already been said on the subject, but rather to challenge some of the prevailing views about alignment and redefine what it can mean in your organization. Specifically, we wish to focus on the issue of aligning the operating systems to the strategic vision. It just makes sense that when the goals of all individuals in an organization are aligned with the overall vision of the company, positive results are more likely to occur. Ensuring those results are achieved, however, only happens when the operations in a company are aligned to its strategic vision.

~

A vision is a statement about where or who you want your company to be in the future as compared with where or who it is today. A compelling vision is a powerful force that creates energy and focus on the direction and future of the organization. A vision statement, in effect, sets the strategic direction for your company, usually over the span of the next three to five years.

Most organizations periodically develop vision statements, sometimes at considerable time and expense. Many have them etched in plaques that hang in their lobbies. Others have them on name cards and stationery. And to their credit, most companies that do create a vision statement also understand the importance, at least in principle, of aligning the rest of the company to their strategic direction in an attempt to translate their vision into action.

The problem is, there is a wide range of theories in existence as to what actually constitutes alignment. As is true so often in business, it can be very difficult to ascertain the value of one approach over another. What we know with certainty from our experience is that, in spite of all good intentions, *the majority of organizations fall **way** short in their attempts to become properly aligned.*

∼

There are unfortunately still some companies where there is little or no effort expended in the direction of lining up daily operations to overall company strategy. In many cases this is due either to the absence of a clear vision statement or the lack of a strategy or plan to achieve the vision. Whatever the specific reason, the reality is that not very many companies today can survive for long using this approach. This is why most companies have at least begun to realize the importance of aligning their strategic business plan to their overall vision. In a progression from least effective to most effective, we discuss these various efforts at alignment as levels I, II, and III.

Level I Alignment

Many organizations are now beginning to attempt to align their resources with their vision. They do this by creating impressive drafts of the strategic direction for the company, a big part of which is the establishment of a vision statement. They may or may not publish it for others to reference, and often discussion about the vision is limited to the upper executives who might have participated in its development. All too often for the majority of the workforce, exposure to the vision amounts to one or more of the following:

- An announcement in the newsletter that the company has a new vision.

- Tent cards placed generously throughout the building reminding employees of the vision.

- A wallet-sized plastic card for all employees to carry on their person with the vision statement written on it.
- Posters around the building displaying the vision.
- A plaque placed on the lobby wall that houses the vision statement.

In all cases, the implicit and often unstated message seems to be, "OK, here's the direction our company is going, now make it happen. Align all of your efforts to the company vision. If everyone does this, we have a decent chance to achieve our vision and meet with success."

The fallacy is that, while this might be the intention of upper management, rarely is it effective. Research indicates that approximately 60-70% of employees asked don't even *know* their company's vision, let alone how to align their work efforts to it!

Level II Alignment

There are, of course, companies that go to the next level and try to line up and coordinate the overall work effort to the corporate vision. Unfortunately, many such attempts are misguided or incomplete, resulting in much chaos, confusion, and wasted resources. Here is a common scenario for how this happens.

XYZ Corporation, a large manufacturing company, schedules a strategic planning retreat with their top executive team, and carefully drafts its vision: **"To be number one in our industry in terms of customer and employee satisfaction."** Thereupon, the executive team is directed to align their respective divisions to the new vision. They return to the plant, and—

- The Vice-President of Human Resources decides to have all of his people develop state-of-the-art training programs. Let's say that part of the training is to upgrade the training on all existing equipment.

- The Vice-President of Operations puts a plan in place for her people to upgrade the quality of their manufacturing and begins to implement a plan to replace 50% of the existing equipment with the newest models.

- The Vice-President of Customer Service decides that his department will implement an extensive customer service strategy which will offer a new and more frequent delivery schedule.

- The Vice-President of Finance decides to reapportion the budget to reduce equipment and training expenditures in preparation for the acquisition of a new facility.

One important question to ask here is, "Has each member of the executive team aligned the strategy of his or her division with the newly developed organizational vision?" The answer is, "yes." Yet another and perhaps more critical question is, "What is the probability that this company will move in the direction of achieving their vision?" The answer is, "little or none." Why not? Because the various efforts to align their divisions with the vision statement are in fact uncoordinated, *misaligned,* and even worse, functioning at cross-purposes.

Now multiply this scenario by the number of employees who have all been directed to develop goals to "support the vision." It is a wonder that any results occur at all, in spite of the fact that everyone is working diligently to become aligned! Far from achieving the desired results, the probability is that this company is in for a year of lower earnings, lost customers, and reduced market share.

~

In one company we worked with, the CEO introduced a Leadership Development session by emphasizing among other things that "It's high time our company started to focus more on getting results!" This is not an uncommon message to hear at the kickoff meeting, by the way, since people are usually brought in to improve outcomes.

After the CEO left the room, one manager who was visibly agitated said, "I feel like I've just been kicked in the shin! Where does he get off telling us that it's about time we start focusing on results? I feel like all we do around here day in and day out is work hard to get results!"

The man clearly had a point. The difference between where the CEO was coming from as compared to the manager's comment relates to the fact that Level II alignment is almost always partial and incomplete, as well as inadequately defined and poorly implemented. Yet this is the norm with Level II alignment. In spite of everyone's good intentions, the results can be almost as scattered as if there were no attempt to align at all. Everyone in the company may well be working hard to achieve results, but they are often going in different directions. The result can be like trying to win a tug-of-war when everyone on your team may be unknowingly pulling on the rope in different directions, as with the left side of the drawing below.

When desired outcomes are thus not achieved, the problem is rarely lack of effort or faulty attitudes, which are common fall-back positions when things go wrong. The problem more often is the absence of a more effective alignment process.

If the alignment process is to be effective, it must involve everyone in the organization, from the boardroom to the boiler room, to ensure that they are all pulling in the same direction. There is no question who will win the tug-of-war when one side is fully aligned and the other is not. The same is true of organizations. Total and complete alignment is so crucial to the success of your company that the Leadership Development Processes we teach address the alignment process first and foremost. Ground zero. Square one.

Level III Alignment

This level represents the alignment process which is embedded in the results-based Leadership Development Processes that we facilitate. It begins with you and your top-level decision makers—your Executive Leadership Team—going through a number of steps together to create the strategic direction for your company.

It is imperative that the strategic direction not be determined by just one individual, say, the president or CEO. Doing so not only sacrifices having access to the insight and wisdom of your other top executives, it also risks not having 100% buy-in from your top level people—an ingredient that is absolutely necessary for your alignment to succeed.

The first task of the Executive Leadership Team is to establish a **vision statement,** which is a statement of who or where you want your company to be in the future. It may or may not be specific; in fact, it usually is not. But it must clearly set direction by pointing to something that your company isn't currently, yet fully intends to become. A brief statement is usually best. Because things change so fast today, we recommend that you conceive of your vision as a three-year plan and not try to project beyond that period of time. Much can happen in three years that might change the strategic direction you will want your company to take in years to come.

Once the vision is complete, the next step is for the Executive Leadership Team to write their **mission statement.** This is a brief statement, again in general terms, of what must be done in the next year to take a significant step in the direction of achieving the three-year vision. In other words, without being too specific, what will your company need to do in the *first* year to get a healthy start on achieving the vision in three years? The mission statement is typically longer than the vision, but brevity is still a good rule to follow.

Next come the **critical success factors,** which are those things that are both necessary and sufficient to achieve the mission. Since the mission is a one-year plan, so are the critical success factors which support the mission (as well as the goals and action steps, which follow). Depending on the size of the company, critical success factors are usually limited to not fewer than four nor more than eight items, and by design are more specific than the mission, yet not as specific as goals.

Goals are then established to accomplish the critical success factors. Goals are more specific than the critical success factors, but not as specific as action plans. There is no limit to the number of goals you must write to achieve each critical success factor. The rule is, "whatever it takes," keeping in mind again that the goals must be both necessary and sufficient to reach the critical success factors.

Finally, each goal will translate to an action plan which is spelled out in one or more specific **action steps: WHO does WHAT by WHEN?**

~

Again: First the Executive Leadership Team establishes a **vision** for the entire organization. Then it must:

- crystallize a **mission** to support that vision

- establish **critical success factors** to support the mission

- create **goals** to support the critical success factors
- write **action steps** to make sure that each goal is achieved.

~

Once your Executive Leadership Team (ELT) has completed their portion of the alignment process, the alignment must then cascade downward throughout the organization until virtually everyone is on board and aligned, from the highest management position to the lowest line job.

The size of your organization will determine how many layers the alignment must work its way through before the process is complete. A larger company, for example, may have to go from:

President & Sr. Vice Presidents (ELT)
to
Vice Presidents
to
Associate/Assistant Vice Presidents
to
Directors
to
Managers
to
Line Workers

The alignment in a smaller company, by contrast, might work its way down from:

President & Vice Presidents (ELT)
to
Managers
to
Line Workers

So again, the steps necessary to put this Level III alignment in place depend on the size and organizational structure of your company. In **every** case, the strategic plan is passed successively from one level to the next until every person in the organization who falls under the scope of the vision is aligned with it. Where each level links with the vision is a matter of what gets passed down from one level to the next, and there is considerable latitude in this regard for how to proceed.

∼

Consider, for example, how the alignment process might work in a smaller company. The Executive Leadership Team may decide to pass their critical success factors to the managers. If so, then the managers would write goals and action steps to support the critical success factors received.

On the other hand, suppose the Executive Leadership Team decides to pass their mission statement to the managers instead. In that event, the managers would write between four and eight critical success factors to support the mission, followed by goals to achieve the critical success factors and action steps to achieve their goals.

In the same fashion, once the managers have completed their strategic plan through to action steps, they must decide what they want to hand down to the employees who report to them. They probably wouldn't start their people at the mission statement, but could well begin with critical success factors or goals. One never passes their own action steps down to the next level, since action steps are written as TO DOs for the person writing them.

It is important to understand that *where you start each successive level doesn't make that much difference.* The crucial elements are: first, that no matter where the connection is made, it all flows back to the same company vision; and second, that the initiatives support each other.

To help understand this better, consider the following three scenarios, again, in the context of a smaller company.

Scenario One

The Executive Leadership Team writes their vision, mission, critical success factors, goals, and action steps. They decide to pass down their **mission statement** for the managers to write their own critical success factors, goals, and action steps.

Scenario Two

The Executive Leadership Team writes their vision, mission, critical success factors, goals, and action steps. They decide to pass down their **critical success factors** for the managers to write their own goals and action steps.

Scenario Three

The Executive Leadership Team writes their vision, mission, critical success factors, goals, and action steps. They decide to pass down their **goals** for the managers to write their own action steps.

The question is, which of these three cases is the most effective way to align your company? The answer is, it really doesn't matter. **All three situations are going to lead to the same place because all three grew out of, and support, the same vision!** Where you start each level in the ongoing alignment process is a matter of practicality and convenience. Most levels of management know intuitively, once they've seen their own plan unfold, exactly where to start the next level down in the organization in order to bring them into full alignment.

~

The point to see here is that total align-ment is a much more involved and calcu-lated process than simply displaying a plaque on the wall, or distributing a vision to everyone in the company with the hope that they will align their goals properly to support it. You must break your vision down into smaller and smaller pieces until everyone in the organization has clear, specific action steps that lead directly to the desired outcomes. When:

- all employees understand their own action steps required to realize the vision; and,

- they are supported with the resources required to do so; and,

- all the processes are in place that ensure productivity, innovation, and speed;

then, and only then, is an organization fully aligned and truly positioned to succeed.

~

When the alignment process is complete, literally everyone in the company has a "to do" list of WHO does WHAT by WHEN. The list is "rolling" and ongoing because it is continually being added to as new goals arise, and subtracted from as goal after goal is accomplished. When all such action steps are complete, the mission has been accomplished, and a giant step has been taken toward achieving the overall vision.

Each planning year begins with a tweaking of the vision statement, an updated mission statement, and the subsequent alignment of all critical success factors, goals, and action steps throughout the company for the coming year. By making alignment an ongoing process such as we've just described, your company moves methodically forward and ever-closer to achieving its vision.

The Level III alignment process, then, is the first of the two most essential Leadership Development Processes that must be implemented and institutionalized in your company if you are serious about getting positive results. By following it, you take the guesswork and the "hope-for-results" mentality out of whether your company actually achieves its desired outcomes. This is because, by virtue of the *power* of the alignment process itself, it will lead systematically, predictably, and scientifically toward the specific desired results you've defined.

— QUESTIONS TO ASK YOURSELF —

1. Do you have a clear statement of Strategic Direction for your company? How recent is it? Was it arrived at mutually by all members of your top executive team? If not, how do you know you have "buy-in"?

2. Do you align everyone in your company to your vision? If so, how do you know it is thorough and complete? If not, can you continue to risk the consequences?

CHAPTER 7

THE LITTLE
ENGINE THAT
COULD

Do you remember the time-honored children's story by this same title? The old engine that normally pulled the train of circus cars broke down one day, and was unable to make it to the other side of the mountain where children were awaiting arrival of the circus. In desperation, the animals on the train were able to recruit a small blue engine to help them out. The little engine recognized that, due to its size, pulling the train up the mountainside would be a very difficult task. But having a positive attitude, he began repeating to himself, *I think I can, I think I can, I think I can, I think I can,* until after hearing himself say it enough, he was finally able to master the mountain and deliver the circus cars to the other side.

∼

Now take a moment and consider the challenges facing you and your organization. The same focus on positive attitudes can help you and everyone in your company realize your goals and vision. Creating a compelling vision is important. Planning is important. Processes are important. Alignment is important. But the bottom line is that you need committed people—like the little engine was committed—to "work" the plan in order for success to become reality. This makes people your number one asset. Your investments in helping them develop their skills AND attitudes must parallel your company's investment in equipment and machinery.

∿

This subject of attitudes cannot be taken lightly. Most experts agree that positive attitudes are an important ingredient of success. Attitudes directly influence behaviors and the corresponding results. Few business leaders would argue the point. And any winning athlete will be among the most vocal champions of the importance of having a winning attitude.

In business, and in life, attitudes directly determine whether an individual turns a problem into an opportunity—or into a crisis. Attitudes affect whether individuals behave in ways that benefit the entire organization or in ways that serve only to protect and maintain their individual fiefdoms. Almost always the attitude of a company representative will determine whether they exceed customer expectations or whether they compound a problem. The truth is that it is not skill, knowledge, or intellect that determines whether the people in your organization seek to reach higher levels of success or remain satisfied with the status quo. It is their attitude.

~

With all the apparent unilateral support regarding the importance of attitudes, it would seem that everyone would have recognized the importance of this issue and that our organizations would be staffed with people who are confident, are focused on solutions, and have positive mental attitudes. As you probably know, this is often not the case. Why not? Because most of us come to the workplace with "baggage" that we've accrued over the years, particularly from early in life. Some experts tell us that as much as 95% of the basic attitudes we carry with us through life are formed by the age of five. Despite the fact that most of us were loved and nurtured as small children, we were nevertheless exposed to so much negativity in our earliest years that there is subsequently a large dose of it embedded in our attitudes by the time we grow to adulthood.

This is evidenced by the fact that one of the first three words we learn to say is "no," along with some rendition of "mommy" and "daddy." The reason is, of course, that children hear the word "no" so often. Parents are not to be blamed for this, since part of good parenting is to set boundaries for one's children, which we do by saying some form of "no" whenever the occasion warrants it. "Don't play in the street," "don't spit out your peas," "don't come to the table without washing your hands," "don't hit your sister." The list goes on endlessly.

By five years of age, we've all been bombarded with countless don'ts, won'ts, can'ts, shouldn'ts, wouldn'ts, and the like, leaving the majority of people in their most formative years with more negative attitudes than positive ones. These negative influences on our thinking eventually make their way into the workplace when we become adults. We've all heard them. "That won't work." "We can't do that." "We've never done it that way before." "It's just another 'flavor of the month'; ignore it and it will go away."

~

Negative attitudes in the workplace are not new phenomena. For reasons just discussed, they've been around since time immemorial. What *is* relatively new is the debilitating effect that negative attitudes can have on business in this age when change happens at such rapid speeds. **Negativity consumes time when time is at an absolute premium!**

If your company is truly going to get results and achieve its vision in today's tough business environment, you must ensure that a process is put in place that consistently transforms negative attitudes into positive ones. Devoid of such a process, attempts to reverse it are usually random and ineffective. For example, the tendency in management is to be critical of other's negativity because, being such a consumer of time and a drain on energy, it is frustrating to deal with. Criticism of those who express negative attitudes, however, isn't the long-term answer. All such criticism is just one more version of negativity, and it serves only to compound the problem.

Some managers try various techniques to keep their people positively motivated as a means to overcome negative attitudes. Unfortunately, positive motivation is difficult to sustain because it is, by nature, so often short-lived. What is needed instead is a *process that will sustain itself* in the face of rapid change, one that will keep people in the "I CAN" or "WE CAN," rather than the "I CAN'T" or "WE CAN'T," mode.

~

The second component of the results-based Leadership Development Process that we help companies implement is specifically designed to sustain positive attitudes in the face of rapid change. We call it the Leadership "Engine." It is supported by and aligned with the structure and strategies of your organization by virtue of the fact that it is the last two steps of your new alignment process. It is, in effect, the goal-setting and goal-achievement process that helps you and all the leaders in your organization plan the steps and pull together the resources that make your vision happen. It is the process that, like "the little engine that could," finally gets the job done. It is, as the saying goes, "where the rubber hits the road," where the best laid plans get converted into actions that are clearly defined and easily measured. It is, in the end, where a company's vision becomes reality.

RESULTS

~

Let's pause and reflect on the subject of "goals" in general before we demonstrate how a goal-achievement process is necessary to convert negative attitudes into positive ones.

Goals are important because they provide direction. It is very difficult to achieve something that is not in one's sight. The absence of having clearly defined personal goals is one of the biggest reasons why so many people go through life feeling frustrated that they never seem to achieve something significant.

In the story of Alice in Wonderland, you may remember, Alice comes upon a Cheshire cat sitting in a tree. She asks the cat, "Which path should I take to get out of here?" The cat asks, "Which way are you going?" Alice replies, "I don't know." The cat says, "Well, then, any path will take you there." Unfortunately, this represents the road taken not only by many individuals, but by many companies, as well.

~

Most business leaders understand the value of setting goals, and they have attempted to encourage their employees to do so. As a result, people frequently do set goals. We are goal-seekers by nature, after all. Think about it. People feel good when they complete a task, get their degree, increase revenues by, say, 17%, or win an athletic contest.

Yet while people are goal-seekers by nature, *we are **not** goal-setters by habit or design.* This is exactly the reason why organizations need a process to make sure that the defined results **do,** in fact, happen.

Again: Everyone knows that it's important to set and achieve goals if they want their company to be successful. Yet too often *setting goals* happens, but achieving them **doesn't,** in spite of everyone's best intentions to do so. Given,

- first, that the human tendency is toward negativity in the face of change; and,

- second, that while individuals are goal-seekers by nature, they are not goal-setters and -achievers by habit;

the crucial question becomes, then, how

does one "habituate" goal planning and goal achievement in their company?

The answer is that **you must implement a goal setting AND goal achievement process.** In doing so you set in motion an "I CAN/WE CAN" methodology that is built into everyone's daily activities. It becomes part of the culture, a way of "positive" thinking that is shared and practiced by every employee in the organization. And this is precisely what the second Leadership Development Process accomplishes.

We address how to institutionalize this process in Chapter 9, but for now it is imperative only that you understand the importance of *implementing* the process and ensuring that it is used on a regular basis. By doing this, you will effectively overwrite the tendency of your employees toward negative attitudes with a positive plan of action that, in short order, becomes the predominant mode of doing business in the face of rapid change.

~

The goal achievement process begins with the formulation of a clear goal. This is the first step toward a commitment to action. The goal must be **S**pecific, **M**easurable, **A**ttainable, **R**ealistically high, and it must have a specific **T**arget date. Many people find it easy to remember the criteria by remembering the acronym: **SMART.**

Your goals can come from any number of sources. For starters, all of the goals that grow out of the alignment process where goals are established to achieve the critical success factors are a given. But your goals can come from other sources, as well. They may be:

- The result of having identified a problem to be solved. Once the problem is clearly defined, the next question is, "What goal do we need to achieve in order to solve this problem?"

- A personal goal related either to one's work or non-work life.

- A team related goal.

Next, you (if it's a personal goal) or your team (if it's a group or team goal) must **spell out the rewards or benefits** for achieving this goal, followed by the **negative consequences** if you don't. These steps in the process help determine its true value. If you are unable to cite benefits for achieving it and consequences if you don't, it probably isn't a worthwhile goal to pursue.

Third, **list every possible obstacle** that might stand in the way of achieving the goal. Ask yourself the question, "If this is really important to me, why haven't I already achieved it?" Fourth, **list the possible solutions** you could use to achieve the stated goal. Make sure that any obstacles you might have listed which truly stand in the way of accomplishing the goal are addressed by these various solutions.

Last, **determine your action plan,** which always ends in WHO does WHAT by WHEN. Start by first determining the WHAT, which is the actual action step. Most, if not all, of your action steps will fall directly out of your list of possible solutions.

Once you've finalized the WHATs, then assign WHO is responsible for driving each action step. The person assigned may do the task herself, or she may delegate it. She may even form a committee or task force to see it through to completion. Regardless, the person whose name has been assigned is ultimately the one who is held accountable to ensure that the action step is completed.

Finally, assign, dates for WHEN each action step must be achieved. Upon its completion, put a check mark beside it. When all action steps for each goal are achieved, record the goal on a master list of goals accomplished. This master list of goals accomplished becomes a running record of a work in progress that tracks your steady movement toward achieving the overall vision.

The goal setting and goal achievement process, that is, the **Leadership Engine,** must become woven into the very fabric of

your organization. It needs to be incorpo-
rated into everyone's daily activities as
part of developing a culture built on positive mental attitudes. It is, as we men-
tioned, the last two steps of the alignment
process as illustrated on pages 72 and 89,
except now it is shown in more detail. In
diagram form it looks like this:

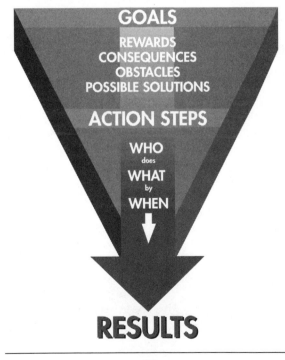

~

In summary, the first of the two essential Leadership Development Processes—i.e. the *alignment process*—helps to establish the vision for where your organization is going. Then it makes sure that virtually everyone is on board and working on the necessary initiatives and assignments to accomplish that vision. Alignment is not a daily process, but happens once a year to define and stay current with your strategic direction.

Then the second Leadership Development Process—the *Leadership Engine*—takes over as the ongoing, even daily, process to make sure that negative attitudes will not prevail in your organization. It also ensures that goals will be set and achieved, and that your vision will actually come to fruition.

In our experience, there is little doubt that establishing an ongoing goal setting and goal achievement process once the alignment process is complete, is the best insurance policy you could possibly have to guarantee your company's ultimate success. It is, in effect, to set in motion a proven system of *Fail-Safe Leadership* that will long endure in your organization.

— QUESTIONS TO ASK YOURSELF —

1. Are negative (or inappropriate) attitudes a problem in your organization? Are there processes in place to convert negative attitudes into positive ones?

2. How would your company benefit if this were possible to do?

3. Many goals programs fail because there are no processes in place to ensure that plans are converted into action. How could such a process help to make your organization stronger?

CHAPTER 8

THE RIGHT FUEL FOR YOUR ENGINE

The heart and soul of any organization consists of its core values. The whole subject of values is a huge one, and aside from some general remarks and the specific piece we're going to talk about here, it clearly falls outside the scope of this work. Fortunately, there are many helpful books written today about the topic, and we certainly encourage your further exploration of the subject.

What is important to say here is that the Leadership Development Processes under discussion *are only as effective as the values that drive them.* Values are to the Leadership Development Processes what gasoline is to an engine. No matter how well built and powerful an engine might otherwise be, it is useless without the proper fuel. It is important, therefore, to ensure that your company's core values are in place to propel your new processes forward.

∼

Most people recognize the importance that value holds in their life. They look for value in the purchases they make. They look for value in the establishments they frequent and in the work they perform. Businesses pride themselves on providing value to their customers and charitable organizations exist to provide value to their patrons and society.

To the point of this book: Organizational values enhance what a company brings to all those who benefit from that company, including the people who work there. They represent an even deeper meaning of the term "value" in the sense that they are an expression of those principles and beliefs that an organization holds to be important.

More specifically, the "core" values of an organization are the standards by which it will exist and operate. The core values of an organization constitute what is known as its "corporate culture," or its "corporate personality." Such values reside in the very "center" of a company to govern the behaviors, decisions, and actions of every individual who works there. They represent the unswerving values to which an organization holds itself accountable. They provide the standard for behavior and the foundation for decisions. In short, *core values are the "lifeblood" of any organization.* Examples of core values are:

- We value people by treating everyone with respect and courtesy.
- Our first concern is our customer.
- We will only work with those clients where we can fulfill a need or provide a valuable service.
- We value exceptional performance and will recognize every employee who exemplifies this value.

~

Some companies are quite aware of their core values because they have taken the time to define them clearly. Your organization may or may not be aware of its own. For purposes of moving forward with the Leadership Development Processes, it really doesn't matter which is the case.

What does matter is that you must now give thought to what values will be needed in your organization to adequately fuel your new processes. You must ask the question, "What must every employee in our company both internalize and espouse as being ultimately important in order for the Leadership Engine to perform optimally?"

Whatever those core values turn out to be, it is the responsibility of the Executive Leadership Team to define them. Doing so must happen immediately following the drafting of the company's vision statement.

∿

We are asked occasionally what values we recommend that companies adopt to drive their new processes forward. Making such a recommendation is difficult to do since there is not one prescribed list of core values that would apply equally to every organization. What's most important is that your Executive Leadership Team decides on those non-negotiable beliefs that you, your senior leaders, and every single employee in your company must commit to and internalize in order to ensure success.

~

We're also sometimes asked, "What distinguishes a value from a behavior?" Actually this is an excellent question because often the two can look very much the same. There is an important difference, however. A behavior is what a person "does." A value, on the other hand, denotes what is believed to be important, which in turn determines "how" one will proceed with regard to his actions. That is, *core values **govern** behavior.*

As an example, let's take a typical core value such as "...honesty and integrity in all dealings..." During a meeting with a potential client, a salesperson has an opportunity to get a contract finalized IF he were to lie about fulfillment dates. Since value governs behavior, the salesperson knows that the only acceptable behavior is truth in all dealings with others. So he is honest with the prospect about the fulfillment dates, even at the risk of not closing the contract. While this Is not always an easy thing to do, it is an example, nonetheless, of how one's value would determine "how" to behave.

Let's take "writing a performance appraisal" as another example. "Writing a performance appraisal" is an action, a behavior, something a person "does." But the company's values about "how" to write that report will influence the behavior. Does the organization value input from others? Will the appraisal be based on results this individual has achieved, attitudes he has demonstrated, risks he has taken, his compliance or non-compliance to policy? The answers depend on the values involved, which, again, will govern the actual behavior of writing the performance appraisal.

~

Having said these things, it is now possible to understand how to distinguish the difference between values and behaviors in an organization. The purpose of vision statements, mission statements, critical success factors, goals, and action steps is to determine the course of **what** everyone in your company is to "do" to ensure that the vision is achieved—*their behaviors.* The purpose of core values is to determine **how** they're going to go about doing it— *their values.*

Again, core values are, in effect, the guiding principles that govern behavior. They are like a circle that encompasses, and therefore influences, all behaviors in an organization.

RESULTS

Without them there is too much latitude for conflicting views on how to go about doing things, the result of which is further misalignment and uncoordinated overall effort. This is why it is incumbent on the

Executive Leadership Team to address the question, "What do we want our people to believe in as the most important values to drive our organization's Leadership Development Processes forward?"

We suggest that you keep the list as short as possible. Three to five is a common number of values to use. These core values, then, must become central to implementing your new processes. We cannot emphasize strongly enough that *they are of equal importance to the vision.* Collectively they become the fuel that powers your company, which is now focused *totally* on getting results, to move forward to eventual victory.

— Questions to Ask Yourself —

1. Have core values been clearly defined in your organization?

2. Are the core values lived by all your employees? If not, at what price?

3. What processes, if any, have you designed to ensure that everyone in your organization owns and lives by these core values?

CHAPTER 9

ALL
OR NOTHING

You want your people to get excited about realizing your company's vision. You want your leaders to be focused on getting results, to have shared commitment, positive mental attitudes, and be focused on being part of the solution rather than part of the problem. It will be necessary, then, that you furnish the tools for them to do so, and those tools are the Leadership Development Processes.

But let's all be clear that these processes are not something that can be done halfway. You must commit to driving these processes home to completion, or they soon fade. "Driving them home to completion" means that not only must they be implemented, they must also become *institutionalized* into the fabric of your organization.

∼

Let's take a step back and put these comments in their proper perspective. You are being asked in this book:

- To redefine what you've always thought about leadership —*that it is related more to the **ability to set goals and achieve results** than to individual leadership qualities.*

- To embrace a new approach to leadership development—*that developing leaders is about developing and following the processes that **lead** to achieving the outcomes you desire.*

- To implement the specific Leadership Development Processes that do, in fact, lead to results, namely *the alignment process and the goal setting/goal achievement process.*

- To revisit the **core values** of your company, and update or revise them where appropriate.

Taken together, these four items are no small task. While they are certainly doable, for most companies they represent a major shift in the prevailing culture. This is not a bad thing, to be sure. Times have changed drastically in recent years, yet most leadership initiatives have not. Therefore making every effort to move your company forward toward a results-based culture is exactly "what the doctor ordered" if you hope to stay one step ahead of the competition.

Yet changing the culture in a company *always* meets with resistance. Plan on it. We human beings are creatures of habit. We don't adapt quickly to change if we

don't have to. We'd rather stay in our com-
fort zones and continue doing things the
way we've always done them. Because this
is true, the collective resistance of your
workforce to the changes you plan to
make in your organization will surely
undermine anything less than a full-blown
commitment from your top executives to
implement and institutionalize the Leadership Development Processes.

In the name of institutionalizing these
processes along with your core values, it
will be necessary, therefore, that you build
them into virtually every conceivable way
that your company does business. To
accomplish this, it is critical that everyone

on the top management team helps to lead that effort. Putting one individual from high in the organization in charge as a "point person" to champion the cause and to coordinate the mechanics of institutionalizing the Leadership Development Processes is always a good call. But ultimately, *every single person* in leadership and management is responsible for—and therefore must be held accountable to—driving these processes into every "nook and cranny" of all divisions and every department in the company.

This means that people must be hired, evaluated, incented, promoted or demoted, and transferred or terminated based on two key factors only: (1) their ability or inability to get results; and (2) their willingness or unwillingness to adhere to the core values.

Furthermore, any functions within the company that do not synchronize with the Leadership Development Processes must be changed so that they do. Meetings, for example, which can so easily become tangential or redundant, must conform to the overarching goal of getting results. All forms that track company processes must be revised and aligned to the Leadership Development Processes, as well. And of prime importance, *every training and development initiative must align to the Leadership Development Processes.*

It is so tempting sometimes when setting up training programs to jump on the bandwagon of the next management or leadership "flavor of the year." Doing so must be avoided at all costs. Only those training programs that enhance and support your new emphasis on institutionalizing a results-based culture deserve attention, and the decision to use them should be made only after close scrutiny to ensure their compatibility with the Leadership Development Processes.

The overall objective is that no matter in what direction each and every member of your organization turns, the central focus must always be to achieve the defined results. Doing so is what leadership is all about, namely:

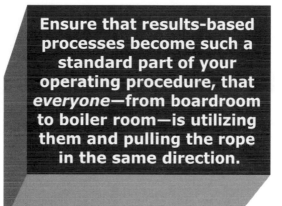

Ensure that results-based processes become such a standard part of your operating procedure, that *everyone*—from boardroom to boiler room—is utilizing them and pulling the rope in the same direction.

When this occurs, your Leadership Development Processes are fully institutionalized, and your company is well on the way to achieving its vision and sustaining its success in the marketplace.

— QUESTIONS TO ASK YOURSELF —

1. Do the people in your organization tend to resist change? If yes, what do you do to counteract such resistance? Does it work?

2. Is there evidence of "flavor of the month" programs in your company? If so, how do you think your employees perceive such efforts?

CHAPTER 10

TREATING
THE
SYMPTOMS

In Chapter 2 the symptoms that made it possible to diagnose whether or not your company has leadership challenges were examined. The point was made that leadership problems, as with any illness, are best resolved by treating the core problem rather than treating the symptoms. That treatment, you've now learned, is to begin implementing and institutionalizing the **Leadership Development Processes** which lead to getting results.

It is time now to take a few moments and reflect back on those same symptoms to see what happens to each of them after the disease has been diagnosed and intervention has begun. Some of the symptoms tend to take on a life of their own and will therefore linger like the aftershocks of an earthquake unless given additional attention. In order to determine what work remains to be done, let's address them in the same order in which they appeared originally.

Excessive Meetings

Too many meetings usually means there is not enough focus on results. Without exception, meetings should happen only when there is a clearly defined purpose and expected outcome. The two purposes for having meetings in a results-based culture are (1) to share information, and (2) to address a task, problem, or goal. In the first case: information will always be important to share in an organization.

The key is to make sure that informational meetings have a focus and a defined outcome.

In the second case, the Leadership Development Engine (Chapter 7) has direct application. What is the goal to be achieved in this meeting? What are the rewards and consequences for achieving that goal? What are the obstacles and possible solutions? WHO does WHAT by WHEN to ensure that the goal is accomplished? End of meeting. No need for further discussion. When people become totally focused on results, the tendency is that there will be fewer meetings. At the same time, when meetings do occur, they will be far more focused and efficient.

There is a simple rule you might want to follow to help ascertain if meetings are appropriate, necessary, and effective. Every meeting should produce a return-on-investment. To determine that number, convert the salary of all participants into a dollar-per-hour figure. Multiply this number by the number of hours the meeting consumes. Always ask, "Will this meeting give us a return on investment (in dollars) that warrants the investment (in time)?" This exercise helps bring awareness to the fact that if a meeting can't be linked to results, then having that meeting is simply not justified.

Preponderance of
Consensus-Driven Decision Making

This relates closely to the matter of excessive meetings. When people aren't sure that they're working on the right things, they naturally want to cover-their-behind by checking to see if they have buy-in from others. Hence the knee-jerk reaction "Let's have a meeting" whenever something comes up.

Largely the need to do so is eliminated once you've completed the alignment process (Chapter 6). When everything everyone does from the top of the organization to the bottom is linked directly to the company's vision, people have much more confidence to decide whether or not they're working on the right things, and the need for consensus building diminishes.

Lack of Personal Accountability

Accountability is a function of tracking and measurement. Once everyone in the organization has clearly written goals and action steps, there is little doubt as to WHO does WHAT by WHEN. Tracking and measurement are part and parcel of the process. Simultaneously, each employee can monitor himself against the completion of his own action steps.

Time-Consuming and/or Meaningless Performance Evaluations

If performance evaluations tend to be lengthy and irrelevant, it simply means that they are not tied to results. This is easily remedied in the context of the Leadership Development Processes. People are evaluated on the results they are expected to achieve based on the goals and action steps to which they've committed. Doing so is straightforward, relatively simple, efficient, and meaningful both for the evaluator and for the person being evaluated.

Communication Problems

There are many different types of communication problems, however two very common types are:

- Insufficient or inaccurate information received—a common protest from the lower levels of an organization;

    or

- Nothing happens with the information sent—an oft-heard complaint from the upper ranks.

Let's look at each. In the first case, the need to receive sufficient and accurate information is usually related to people needing to know what they're supposed to be doing. Proper alignment addresses the majority of such situations.

In the second instance, when information sent is not acted upon, it is usually due to the absence of a specific process to convert the information sent into action. In the Leadership Development Processes, this conversion factor is clearly present in the form of the Leadership Engine.

Difficulty Terminating Poor Performers

Results are everything. When a person consistently does not get results, intervention is necessary. This relates to what we said in Chapter 4: *First define results, then grow people to ensure those results.* When someone is not achieving results, the best initial intervention is assessment and development. The question must be asked, "What about this person is getting in the way of accomplishing his or her goals?"

If the lack of results persists after the proper steps for intervention have been taken, then transfer or termination may be in order. Making the decision to do so is neither subjective nor difficult when the time comes. Performance is all measured and tracked—i.e. documented—in that person's rolling action list.

Misalignment/Lack of Coordinated Effort

This symptom totally disappears once the annual alignment process is fully implemented.

Personality Conflicts and/or Power Struggles

There is a simple rule about this matter: *when effective processes are missing, personalities take over.* In other words, if you don't have processes that specify "what to do" and "how to do it," then decisions become a matter of "will" rather than "process." This is when egos come to the fore and power struggles begin. Implementation of the Leadership Development Processes goes a long way toward remedying this problem.

Difficulty Keeping Employees Motivated

People are goal seekers by nature. This means that by and large we enjoy following a process for setting and reaching goals. When the work environment is such that goal setting and goal achievement are a fundamental part of the corporate tapestry, people have daily opportunities to experience goal achievement. The result is that employees tend to motivate themselves, which is the atmosphere management should always be striving to achieve.

Unacceptable Results

Never again! This entire approach is about achieving results, and nothing else.

Time Management Problems

The greatest consumer of employee time is meetings. Develop the proper meeting processes, and the vast majority of time management problems go away. To assist in this regard, we recommend the following guidelines to help manage meeting times:

- Sr. Level Management: 80-100% of time spent in meetings.
- Associate or Assistant Vice Presidents: 70-90%
- Directors: 60-80%
- Managers: 40-60%
- Supervisors: 20-40%
- Line Workers: 0-30%, depending on the industry (line employees in an information technology department, for example, will obviously need to dedicate more time to meetings than would production line workers)

For the majority of companies, these guidelines represent considerably less time spent in meetings than is usual and customary. We quite often hear comments from people even at the Director and Manager levels like, "If I get two or three hours a week when I'm not in meetings, I'm lucky, and even then it's usually because of cancellations." There will be no excuse for such assaults on one's use of time once your results-based culture is fully in place.

Reactive Rather Than Proactive Thinking

Reactive thinking results from inade-quate planning. When people don't know what to do, they tend to "wait and see," which feels like the safest course to follow. Proper alignment from vision to action steps for everyone in the company allows for and encourages proactive behavior.

Micro-Management

Micro-management occurs when peo-ple are concerned that their direct reports are either not working on the right things, or not in the right ways. In a company that is aligned from top to bottom, these fears are typically relaxed because the right things to work on (goals and action plans), as well as the right ways to work on them (values), are clearly defined at every level of the organization.

Can't Do Attitudes

This problem largely goes away once you've fully implemented the *"I CAN"* Leadership Engine.

Chronically Sagging Sales

The sales department is no different than any other division of the company. Develop a plan; align all efforts to that plan; set goals and action steps to achieve the desired results; and bingo, results happen. This does not mean that sales never again dip or slow down, since clearly external factors such as the economy or new competition on the scene can cause blips on the sales growth chart. The question here is whether or not sagging sales are *chronic.* If so, the answer is to implement the Leadership Development Processes.

Unproductive Teams and/or Ineffective Teamwork

Teams that do not function well are not properly focused on results. This is due typically to one of three factors: lack of alignment between team goals and company goals; excessive time spent in discussions either to build consensus or otherwise wander off on tangents; or lack of team accountability for results. Clearly, the Leadership Development Processes remedy all three situations.

Duplication of Effort

Anytime efforts are duplicated, it is the predictable consequence of improper alignment. Get everyone pulling on the rope in the same direction, and duplication of effort disappears.

High Staff Turnover

People leave companies for a variety of reasons. What keeps the majority of employees happy is the opportunity to get their needs met at work. Most of those needs fit into one or two of five categories:

Achievement
Challenge
Belonging
Recognition
Advancement

In a results-based culture, the opportunity to meet these needs are ever-present. Those who best get results will experience ample *Achievement* and *Challenge;* they will feel that they *Belong* to an aligned company with common goals, common processes, common language, common values, and a common direction; they will be *Recognized* in proportion to goal achievement; and those who do it best will have plenty of opportunity for *Advancement.*

Failure to Achieve Quality Standards

Quality issues go away once you implement the Leadership Development Processes. Quality is a function of bringing your defined outcomes to completion. What is it concerning quality that you want to achieve? Once that is defined, you can set goals and action steps that lead to the desired result.

Fear of Making Decisions

This relates directly to the preponderance of consensus-driven decision making. If one isn't sure that she is doing the right things, she is afraid to act until there is sufficient buy-in and support from others. In a fully aligned organization, indecision tends to evaporate. Everyone knows exactly what they are expected to do. As a result, decision making becomes straightforward and routine, and purposeful action rather than random reaction prevails.

∼

Again, first the Leadership Development Processes must be put in place to treat the root cause of the leadership challenges in your company. Once that is done, then the symptoms must be revisited and corrected. Subsequent to that, you are well on your way to having institutionalized a results-based culture in your organization that will lead consistently and repeatedly to your desired outcomes.

— QUESTIONS TO ASK YOURSELF —

1. What would it be like if your organization had only the right number and kinds of meetings, nobody was trying to cover his backside, everyone was accountable, performance evaluations were related directly to the achievement of results, communication problems were kept to a minimum, poor performers were transferred or terminated, all effort was aligned and coordinated, personality conflicts and power struggles were nearly nonexistent, employees were perpetually motivated, there were no time management problems, all thinking was proactive rather than reactive, can't do attitudes disappeared, sales were consistently high, teams were productive and effective, staff turnover was low, quality standards were regularly achieved, and people weren't afraid to take risks and make decisions? If this doesn't describe your company currently—what can you do to make it happen?

CHAPTER 11

IN CONCLUSION

So there you have it—*Fail-Safe Leadership,* and what you can do to correct the leadership challenges in your organization.

Leadership is about results, and leadership development is about creating an environment in which the leaders of your organization—essentially **everyone** under the new definition—recognize their role and responsibility in achieving the goals to which they commit. It is about providing them with the Leadership Development Processes that will enable them to develop the necessary skills, and about implementing those processes to ensure that results are, in fact, achieved.

In the absence of such processes, there will likely be various uncoordinated attempts to define and grow "leaders" in your company. And the chances are high that such efforts will not be focused on the right issues, nor will they be properly aligned in the ways necessary to make your overarching strategy become reality. The results of such hasty or sloppy initiatives are all too often limited, and sometimes can actually be negative.

To ensure the success of your initiatives AND of your future, there must be 100% commitment on the part of senior management to take action. Specifically, they must commit to a comprehensive and effective Leadership Development Process that (a) aligns people, processes, and strategy; (b) incorporates the development of skills, attitudes, and the ability to set and achieve goals; and (c) is sustainable over time.

Anything less than this risks falling into the "flavor of the month" morgue. In fact, when organizational initiatives appear and disappear on a regular basis with very little lasting positive change, people tend to become "hardened" against *all* attempts at improvement, making it increasingly difficult to effect the changes necessary to succeed. In addition, there will be a growing sense of futility amongst your leaders because the processes won't be in place to take the company where you want it to go. They would be like prize fighters who are told to come out fighting, even though both hands are tied behind their backs.

~

The world of business is spinning faster every day. We all know that to be the case. Competition is getting keener by the hour. The window of time to take advantage of new opportunities continues to get smaller, being measured sometimes now in "nanoseconds." Every company that plans to survive and excel into the future must get its "ducks in a row" and move forward with a single-mindedness of purpose toward the achievement of its defined outcomes.

Traditionally too many organizations have viewed leadership development as a discretionary "training" program. Today they are beginning to recognize that people are an organization's greatest asset, and that developing their people—*and the Leadership Development Processes their people need in order to succeed*—is anything *but* a discretionary expense. To the contrary, it is actually an investment that yields a huge return.

∿

The message is clear. If your organization suffers from a leadership problem and you do nothing to correct it, your success is questionable. Imagine that a doctor diagnoses you with a serious illness. Your two choices are, do nothing and probably die from it, or take aggressive action to get back on the road to optimal health. What would you do? If there are leadership challenges in your company, you have, in effect, the same choices.

In order for you to lead your company on the road to victory, *you must empower your people with the processes that allow them to lead,* as well. When you do so, literally **everyone in your organization becomes a leader**. There is no other way. And for everyone to be a leader, the tools every leader needs—*some* form of Leadership Development Processes—must be at their disposal to **follow.**

Without those processes, leaders can't help but fail to lead, making your chances for victory in today's business climate increasingly doubtful. With the Leadership Development Processes fully in place, however, you develop a fail-safe approach to leadership where *leaders* **can**—*and* **do**—*lead,* and victory for your company in the marketplace is ensured.

— QUESTIONS TO ASK YOURSELF —

1. Make two lists: one for the reasons to move forward putting the Leadership Development Processes in place, and the other for the reasons to wait.

2. When you compare these two lists, what do you think is the best decision for the overall success of your organization?

ABOUT THE AUTHORS AND THEIR COMPANIES

ABOUT
THE AUTHORS

Dr. David G. Mutchler

David is the President and CEO of Leadership Development Systems, LLC, a firm that provides leadership services to a wide range of businesses. He is an affiliate of Resource Associates Corporation, and has trained and consulted locally, nationally, and internationally in such industries as Information Technologies, Radio and Television, Printing, Automotive, Utilities, Construction, Engineering, Publishing, Real Estate, Packaging, Petroleum, Medical,

Legal, Financial, Manufacturing, Telecommunications, Insurance, Industrial Equipment, and a host of wholesale and retail businesses.

David began his career as an educator at the secondary, and later at the college, levels. He also coached football for many years where he built several championship teams. After completing his doctorate in psychology, he founded and directed a private counseling agency. Since 1990 he has combined his professional experiences as teacher, athletic coach, and counselor to become a corporate consultant, coach, and facilitator where he now specializes in leadership process development, goal achievement, management training, and individual executive leadership development. David is a highly sought after speaker and seminar leader, and also has coauthored two previous books on leadership.

Linda L. Martin
(1947–2002)

Linda was the President and CEO of Resource Associates Corporation (RAC) from the time she founded it in 1978 until 2002. RAC is an international personal and organizational development firm that is headquartered in Reading, Pennsylvania. RAC is recognized as a leader in the field of performance improvement and leadership development. In the twenty-three years since its inception, RAC has experienced consistent upward growth, including developing a network of several hundred highly skilled specialists who facilitate the RAC processes to produce measurable results for their clients, both individually and organizationally.

Linda spent over thirty-five years in the training and development field, personally working with clients in a wide range of business and industry, not-for-profit organizations, education, and government. Her books, manuals, programs, and processes are presently being used by hundreds of thousands of people all over the world. In addition to her writing, she was also a speaker and lecturer on a wide range of business and achievement issues, and personally coached many executives and business leaders. She was an active member of the boards of Total Quality Institute and the Florida Tax Watch, and was a member of several business organizations.

ABOUT LEADERSHIP DEVELOPMENT SYSTEMS, LLC

Leadership Development Systems, LLC is a training and development firm that specializes in helping companies achieve the outcomes they desire in an efficient and cost effective manner. Largely this involves assisting organizations to implement and institutionalize the Leadership Development Processes that are proven to lead to accomplishing desired results.

The Leadership Development Processes have application in every division and at every level of an organization regardless of the industry involved. The greatest overall effect occurs when those processes begin at the top and cascade their way downward until they have become institutionalized into the entire fabric of a company.

Leadership Development Systems, LLC emphasizes the importance of customizing the leadership processes to fit a company's specific needs, and in helping facilitate, mentor, and coach the actual implementation of the processes from start to finish on however large or small a scale as is appropriate to the situation.

Leadership Development Systems, LLC
can be contacted at:

LEADERSHIP DEVELOPMENT SYSTEMS, LLC
2035 28th Street SE, Suite P
Grand Rapids, Michigan 49508
616.452.3838
800.452.3896
Fax 616.452.0728
Email:
dmutchler@lds-llc.com

For more information, visit our website at:
www.lds-llc.com

ABOUT RESOURCE ASSOCIATES CORPORATION

Resource Associates Corporation (RAC) is an international personal and organizational development firm headquartered in Reading, Pennsylvania. RAC is a recognized leader in helping organizations create and sustain a competitive advantage. It provides a wide range of materials and processes that are tailor-designed to meet the needs of each client. In addition to

Leadership Development and Executive Leadership Development, other core competencies include Strategic Thinking and Business Planning, Management Development, Sales Improvement, Customer Service, and Time Strategies.

In the twenty-three years since its inception, RAC has worked with clients that include major corporations, not-for-profit foundations, government agencies, and small family-owned businesses. It is represented in virtually every state in the United States, as well as in Canada, Hong Kong, South America, and Mexico.

Resource Associates Corporation can be
contacted at:

RESOURCE ASSOCIATES CORPORATION
31 Hickory Road
Mohnton, PA 19540
800.762.6227
Fax 610.775.9686
Email:
info@ResourceAssociatesCorp.com

For more information, visit our website at:
www.ResourceAssociatesCorp.com